W9-AZX-557

Forecasts

by Kristin Schuetz

BELLWETHER MEDIA • MINNEAPOLIS, MN

Note to Librarians, Teachers, and Parents:

Blastoff! Readers are carefully developed by literacy experts and combine standards-based content with developmentally appropriate text.

Level 1 provides the most support through repetition of high-frequency words, light text, predictable sentence patterns, and strong visual support.

Level 2 offers early readers a bit more challenge through varied simple sentences, increased text load, and less repetition of high-frequency words.

Level 3 advances early-fluent readers toward fluency through increased text and concept load, less reliance on visuals, longer sentences, and more literary language.

Level 4 builds reading stamina by providing more text per page, increased use of punctuation, greater variation in sentence patterns, and increasingly challenging vocabulary.

Level 5 encourages children to move from "learning to read" to "reading to learn" by providing even more text, varied writing styles, and less familiar topics.

Whichever book is right for your reader, Blastoff! Readers are the perfect books to build confidence and encourage a love of reading that will last a lifetime!

This edition first published in 2016 by Bellwether Media, Inc.

No part of this publication may be reproduced in whole or in part without written permission of the publisher. For information regarding permission, write to Bellwether Media, Inc., Attention: Permissions Department, 5357 Penn Avenue South, Minneapolis, MN 55419.

Library of Congress Cataloging-in-Publication Data

Schuetz, Kristin.
   Forecasts / by Kristin Schuetz.
      pages cm – (Blastoff! Readers: Understanding Weather)
   Summary: "Relevant images match informative text in this introduction to forecasts. Intended for students in kindergarten through third grade"–Provided by publisher.
   Audience: Ages 5-8
   Audience: K to grade 3
   Includes bibliographical references and index.
   ISBN 978-1-62617-251-7 (hardcover: alk. paper)
   1. Weather forecasting–Juvenile literature. 2. Weather–Juvenile literature. I. Title.
   QC995.43.S38 2016
   551.63–dc23
                                        2015004208

Printed in the United States of America, North Mankato, MN.

Table of **Contents**

What Is a Forecast?

Meteorologists help to prepare us for the coming day, week, or month.

SAT

HIGH 64   LOW 53

SUN

HIGH 68   LOW 55

They tell us what they think the weather will be like. This is called a forecast.

A forecast is a number of guesses based on facts.

The guesses guide how we dress. They help us plan when to be outside.

THUR
61

MON

HIGH
60

LOW
52

Forecasts **predict** high and low **temperatures**.

HEAT WAVE

	MON	TUE	WED	THUR	FRI	SAT	SUN
HIGH	60	69	81	95	89	81	76
LOW	52	60	72	80	79	73	65

	MON	TUE	WED	THUR	FRI	SAT	SUN
HIGH	60	51	42	29	32	39	46
LOW	52	42	36	19	24	29	37

COLD SPELL

A weekly or monthly forecast can show **heat waves** and **cold spells**.

A forecast will tell you if hot days will be **humid**.

HOT AND HUMID

MON

HIGH
93

LOW
84

Meteorologists look at how much **water vapor** will be in the air.

They also look at how the wind will act. Will it move fast? In which direction will it blow?

TUE **STRONG WINDS**

HIGH
28

LOW
17

Wind can make a temperature feel colder. This is called **windchill**.

A forecast tells if rain, snow, or other **precipitation** is on the way.

SEVERE WEATHER

WED

HIGH
89

LOW
77

It warns about the danger of **severe weather**.

Cloud cover is
predicted, too.

THUR

PARTLY
CLOUDY

HIGH
79

LOW
71

Will the sky be clear and blue?
Will it be gray and stormy?

Tools for Making Forecasts

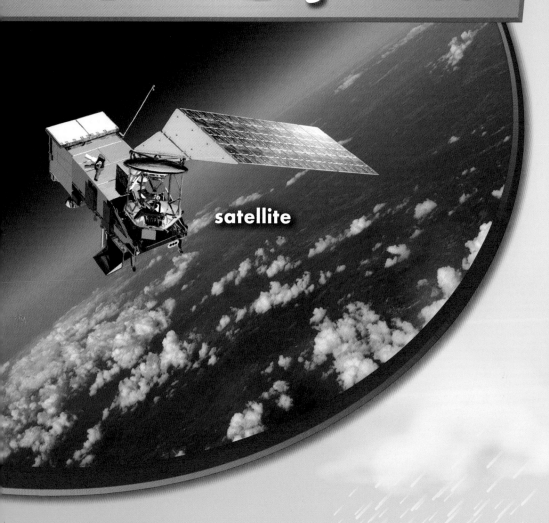

satellite

Meteorologists use many tools to predict the weather. **Satellites** send information from space.

Radar spots moving precipitation.

radar

Forecasts give us a good idea
of what to expect. However, the
weather can surprise us.

It never hurts to
have a hat or an
umbrella along!

Glossary

cloud cover–the amount of sky covered by clouds

cold spells–periods of very cold weather

heat waves–periods of very warm weather

humid–damp or moist

meteorologists–people who study and predict the weather

precipitation–water that falls from the sky as rain, hail, or snow

predict–to tell ahead of time what might happen

radar–a tool that sends out radio waves to collect weather data

satellites–tools that move around in space to collect weather data

severe weather–bad weather that can harm land, buildings, and people

temperatures–measures of how hot or cold it is outside

water vapor–water in the form of a gas

windchill–how cold the temperature really feels due to the wind

To Learn More

AT THE LIBRARY

Barrett, Judi. *Cloudy With a Chance of Meatballs.* New York, N.Y.: Atheneum Books for Young Readers, 1982.

DeWitt, Lynda. *What Will the Weather Be?* New York, N.Y.: HarperCollins, 1991.

Kudlinski, Kathleen V. *Boy, Were We Wrong About the Weather!* New York, N.Y.: Dial Books for Young Readers, 2014.

ON THE WEB

Learning more about forecasts is as easy as 1, 2, 3.

1. Go to www.factsurfer.com.

2. Enter "forecasts" into the search box.

3. Click the "Surf" button and you will see a list of related web sites.

With factsurfer.com, finding more information is just a click away.

Index